To my wonderful editors Juliana McIntyre and Kelly Swanson
—E. J.

For Marly, Brooke, and Jocelyn
—J. D. E.

Turn of the Century

Ellen Jackson

Illustrated by Jan Davey Ellis

Charlesbridge

A new century . . .

and a new millennium stretch before us. We are living at an exciting time, a time when people look ahead and imagine what the future will bring. But the change of the millennium is also a time to look back over the last one thousand years to see how far we have come.

This book shines a spotlight on eleven children living in England or America, each from a different century. It shows how the lives of children in the past were both similar to and different from those of children today.

How did children live during the last one thousand years? If you see a painting that is very old, you may notice that children look like small adults and not like children at all. Long ago, children were dressed as adults, and many were expected to work alongside adults, learning a trade at a very young age.

In other ways, though, the daily lives of children in former centuries were very much like those of modern children. Some children blew bubbles, spun tops, or played board games. Others played blindman's bluff and hide-and-seek. And, of course, in every century children needed food, warmth, laughter, and love—just as they still do.

—Ellen Jackson

John, Son of Stephen
A Ten-Year-Old Peasant Boy

Today is the twenty-fifth day of March, the first day of the year 1000. So says the priest, but I know not of such things.

I, John, live in the village of Nottingwood in Angle-land. My family works the land six days a week and gives our lord a portion of the crops. Our lord owns furs, jewelry, silver coins, and one book—a Bible copied by monks on fine sheepskin. I have no use for books as I cannot read.

I own only the clothes on my back, and they once belonged to my grandfather. My family and I live in a two-room hut made of mud, straw, and animal hair. We sleep together on a big straw mattress. The pigs and chickens sleep in the other room. In the winter we let Enid the cow come in to help keep us warm.

Today we sang a planting song as we plowed the land. If all goes well, we shall have wheat, barley, and beans to keep us alive next winter.

IN THE YEAR 1000 . . .

~ Books are rare and valuable. Many people have
  never seen one.
~ People use sundials to tell time, but many do not
  know the date or the year.
~ Most poor people work from dawn to dusk farming a
  small plot of land. Children work alongside their parents.
~ Families are big. Women often have ten children or more, but
  many children die before their seventh birthday.
~ Many people live their entire lives without
  handling money.
~ Paper and gunpowder are unknown in
  England, which is called Angle-land.
~ The New Year begins on March
  25, not on January 1.

Eleanor
A Nine-Year-Old Lady

'Tis New Year's Day, 1100, and the nuns at Wilton Abbey and their students (I am one) greeted the new year with a dinner of herring pie, turnips, and pease pottage. We ate in silence, as usual. I must ask the nuns to pass the herring pie by putting my hands together and wiggling them like a fish's tail.

Here at the nunnery we rise in the middle of the night for singing and prayers. Then we return to bed and sleep until dawn. We spend the rest of each day in work, study, and prayer. Sometimes I help with the farm chores. Yesterday I repaired the nuns' clothes and picked burrs out of a basket of sheep's wool.

I already know how to fly falcons and play chess, but the nuns will teach me to read and write Latin, to draw, to embroider, and to prepare herbs and medicines. I hope my husband-to-be, Lord Norbert, will be happy with my skills. We have been betrothed since I was seven and will marry before I am fifteen.

IN THE YEAR 1100 . . .

~ Upper-class girls are educated in nunneries or in nearby manors, where they learn how to manage a household.

~ Girls are trained to care for the sick. There are almost no doctors.

~ Many people believe in witches, unicorns, monsters, and magic.

~ Most people never travel. They live, marry, and die within a few miles of the place where they were born.

~ Parents arrange the marriages of their children. Many upper-class girls are betrothed, or engaged, at age six or seven but do not meet their husbands until shortly before their weddings.

Geoffrey, A Ten-Year-Old Page

Greetings! I, Geoffrey, salute the year 1200! At Berwick Castle, where I am a page to my uncle, I am learning manners, the knightly code of honor, and jousting. Tuesday last, I knocked Robert from his horse with one thrust of my lance. Today we played dice and pitch-and-toss, as Robert is still smarting from my blow.

Oh, how I long to see faraway places such as Alexandria and Damascus! When I go on a crusade, I shall ride a chestnut horse decked in bells and silks. Musicians will play harps and trumpets and wish me Godspeed.

My uncle says that many go but few return. He talks of blood, hunger, and the eating of donkey meat. Yet he came back from the Holy Land with velvet hangings and copper pots and many wonderful new foods and spices, such as figs, almonds, saffron, and ginger. He also brought back a wondrous glass mirror for my grandfather. I do not think Grandfather likes what he sees, as he is almost forty and toothless.

In the Year 1200 . . .

- Upper-class boys are educated in the arts of war. Only a few upper-class children are taught to read.
- Many people do not live past the age of thirty-five or forty.
- The ship's compass is beginning to be used in Europe.
- Crusaders who fought the Turks in Jerusalem have returned to England bringing many new foods, such as oranges, peaches, apricots, and sugar.
- Children play dice and board games, including a game called tables, a form of backgammon.

Rhys
An Eight-Year-Old Merchant's Son

It is the year 1300. I, Rhys, the merchant's son, pray this new year brings better luck than this day has brought to me.

On my way to school at Saint Paul's, my hose and shoes were splattered when a maid tossed slops into the street. I shook my fist at her. Next a goat knocked my hand, and I lost my cow's horn filled with ink.

At school I knelt and said my Hail Mary. I made a pen by cutting a quill feather with my knife. Then I borrowed ink from Nicholas. I remembered the words to the Lord's Prayer when asked to recite, but I forgot one of the seven deadly sins. The master rapped my knuckles.

There were maggots in the meat at lunch. It is the kitchen boy's task to pick them out, but he had run off to view a hanging.

Well, no matter. Tomorrow is a festival day. I shall see the story of Noah's flood played by a troupe of actors. Then I shall buy a sweet apple tart and forget this day.

IN THE YEAR 1300 ...

- London has a population of forty thousand people. Many who live in the city keep horses, cattle, pigs, and poultry.
- Both children and grown-ups attend public hangings.
- Mechanical clocks are beginning to be used in Europe.
- At Saint Paul's School in London, 150 boys are educated in one large room. The schoolmaster sits in a high chair holding a rod. Boys who forget their lessons are beaten.
- People spill slops and refuse of all kinds into the gutters, and visitors to London complain of the smell.
- Everyone, including children, drinks ale because the water is not fit to drink.

Alice
A Ten-Year-Old Chambermaid

On this first day of the year 1400, I awoke at dawn. I placed a chair before the fire with a cushion for my lady's feet and pulled back the curtains of the bed, saying, "My lady, what robe or gown does it please you to wear today?"

Lady Margaret chose a gown trimmed with fur and a strand of coral beads. I helped her dress. Then I beat the featherbed. I am needed in the kitchen this afternoon. Later I shall sneak into the great hall and listen to the minstrels and their lively talk. Tonight some traveling players will perform the story of Troy, and there will be much feasting and laughter.

When it is time to retire, I shall undress Lady Margaret, turn back the sheet, drive out the dog and cat, and set the chamber pot ready. Lady Margaret is pleased with me and seldom pulls my hair.

Though I cannot read and write, I am clean and do not hiccup, scratch, or blow my nose too loudly. I have not had the smallpox, and my face is unmarked. Felix, the miller's son, says I am as pretty as a dove, and I well believe it.

IN THE YEAR 1400 . . .

~ In manor houses meals are announced with a blast from a horn. People sit on benches and use pieces of flat bread for plates. Most people eat with their fingers.

~ Girls, as well as boys, are sent out to work at an early age. Servants are fed and clothed, and it is expected that they will remain unmarried.

~ Tapestries on the walls of manor houses keep out the drafts. Candles and smoky torches dipped in mutton fat provide light.

~ Children have few toys. They play games similar to hide-and-seek and follow the leader. They spin tops, blow soap bubbles, and play with shells and stones.

Annabelle Hugh
An Eight-Year-Old Daughter of an Earl

Today I rose at daybreak, gave thanks to God, and received my father's blessing for the New Year, 1600.

I worked at my Latin and French in the morning and played upon my lute. I am also learning needlework, though I find it dull.

The barber came to trim my father's beard and treat him for baldness, using a mixture of garlic, honey, and wormwood. After three such treatments, however, I see no difference. The barber also pulled my brother's tooth.

After noon Lydia and I had a game of tenpins. Then we went by coach to the south side of London to see a pageant.

In the evening we read the Scriptures before dining. The milk is sour again. The cook says 'tis witches' work. She saw an old woman give this house the evil eye yesterday.

At table my mother uses a fork to serve herself, as the Italians do. And my father has taken up a most peculiar custom from the West Indies. After dining, he draws tobacco smoke into his mouth and lungs–for what purpose, I cannot say!

IN THE YEAR 1600 . . .

- The houses of the rich now have chimneys, gardens, gravel walks, and fishponds. Plates are made of silver and pewter. Forks are known but not commonly used.
- New theaters have been built in London, and a play can be seen for a penny or two.
- A number of people, usually women of the lower classes, are tried as witches and put to death.
- Plants from the New World, such as tobacco and potatoes, have recently been introduced into England.
- Barbers cut hair, but they also pull teeth and perform minor surgery.

Roger Dabbs
A Seven-Year-Old Massachusetts Boy

Today the bells rang at daybreak and we welcomed the New Year, 1700. I began the day by helping my mother make soap and candles. I cut wicks while she poured boiling fat into the molds.

On the way to school, I passed the wharf and saw my friend Josiah. We played pirates on the ships, as no one was around to chase us away.

At school we read from the **New England Primer.** We are learning to write a good, clear hand. Josiah could not do his sums and had to wear the dunce cap.

After school Josiah and I wandered through the streets and frightened some pigs rooting in the garbage.

We had baked beans and brown bread for dinner. When my father snored at the table, I put on his wig and spectacles and made my sister laugh. Mother said I am a saucy boy who needs a good whipping.

When I am older, I will be apprenticed to a silversmith. I shall stoke the furnace, sweep the floor, and learn to make teapots, buckles, and lockets. It is a trade that shall suit me.

In the Year 1700 . . .

∼ About 6,700 people live in Boston, the largest town in North America. Many people have books in their homes, such as the Bible and *Pilgrim's Progress*.

∼ Both boys and girls go to the new free schools. Business records, letters, and reports are handwritten, and it is very important for children to learn good penmanship.

∼ Many boys are apprenticed at age twelve or thirteen. For seven years they are expected to work for a master while they learn a trade.

∼ Pocket watches, waterproof umbrellas, and slide rules are now available, and the clarinet has just been invented. Merry-go-rounds are becoming very popular in Europe.

2007
608,352
———
1700
6,700

Rebecca Foster
A Seven-Year-Old Kentucky Girl

Today is the first day of the 1800s. I say it is the new century, but Pa says we must wait another year for that. Old Mr. Wilson came by last night with his fiddle and some fine tunes. We laughed when he took out his new false teeth to show us how they work!

Ma made corn dumplings with blackberry jelly, and we played blindman's bluff. At midnight all the men fired their pistols.

It's back to the usual chores today. The fire is sputtering like an angry hen, and I have stockings to knit and butter to churn before dinner.

My hands are red and rough from washing in icy water—and from carrying hot potatoes five miles to school. The potatoes keep my hands warm inside my mittens and make a good noontime meal. But I can't go to school this week, for I have much spinning and weaving to do. Perhaps the boys will go. It's more important for them to get book learning.

I need to go to the smokehouse to get a ham. Today is a gloomy day, and I'm afraid I shall fancy an Indian or a bear behind every bush!

IN THE YEAR 1800 . . .

~ Frontier children often stay home from school to help in the fields or in the house.

~ On the frontier, people live in log cabins chinked with clay. Some families also have a smokehouse, a supply shed, and a dairy.

~ Porcelain false teeth, carbonated water, steam engines, pianos, and baby carriages are appearing. A vaccine for smallpox is now available.

~ A new snack, created when the Earl of Sandwich placed meat and cheese between two slices of bread, is becoming popular.

~ About one fourth of the white families in the southern United States own slaves. People from every region are beginning to argue about the issue of slavery.

Emily Prescott
An Eight-Year-Old Pennsylvania Girl

This New Year's Day, 1900, has been a most pleasant one. When I rose, Papa was in the cellar shoveling coal into the furnace to warm the house. I fetched some firewood for the stove.

After breakfast Mama read the newspaper, and I looked at the comic strips. "The Katzenjammer Kids" is my favorite.

Mama reminded me that Uncle Albert was arriving on the train today, and I should put on my new petticoat and dress. Then Papa harnessed the horses to the buggy, and we drove to the depot.

After we greeted my uncle, Papa proposed a special treat–ice cream! Mama had vanilla, and I tried chocolate. It was delicious.

Uncle Albert told us about his horseless carriage. It goes twenty-five miles an hour–so fast that he wears goggles to keep the dust out of his eyes! He said he would take me for a ride in the summer.

In the evening Papa put a record on the phonograph and wound it with a crank. Then we all danced. It was a fine day, to be sure.

In the Year 1900 . . .

- Many houses have electricity, but most do not have indoor plumbing. Water is heated on wood-burning stoves for cooking and bathing. Coal is burned in furnaces for household heating.
- Telephones, automobiles, cameras, and bicycles are beginning to appear. People can now travel long distances by train.
- There are hospitals in some cities, but doctors do not have effective treatments for most diseases. Aspirin and antibiotics are unknown.
- Many people now enjoy going to the movies. A motion picture lasts about twenty minutes and has no sound.
- Soda fountains are becoming popular. Ice cream is available in several flavors, including vanilla, strawberry, chocolate, cherry, and tutti-frutti.

John Stevenson
A Ten-Year-Old California Boy

Today is January 1, the first day of the year 2000! Last night I watched coverage of New Year's celebrations in South America, France, and Japan on TV. People greeted the new millennium with fireworks, music, and dancing. Dad made microwave popcorn, and we called my sister Lisa in Australia to wish her a happy turn of the century.

This afternoon my friend Mark and I went skateboarding. Then we ate chocolate-chip banana ice cream in his new tree house. Mark taped a picture of a mountain gorilla on the wall. He says he's going to call his tree house the Monkey House. Oh, brother!

Later Mom and I went to the recycling center. When we came home, I got on the Internet and talked to my friend Joey in England. He sent me some cool close-up pictures of Saturn.

Dad and I set the table while we listened to the evening news. One story was about pollution and another was about gangs. I wish the world didn't have so many problems. But then I remember that a thousand years ago most people couldn't even read. We've come a long, long way.

It's a new millennium, and I can't wait to see what comes next!

In the Year 2000 . . .

~ New communications and transportation systems allow
  people in different parts of the world to talk to one
  another and ship goods back and forth.

~ Pollution and the destruction of natural resources are
  major problems. Many people recycle plastic,
  newspaper, and aluminum in their communities.

~ New weapons, such as nuclear bombs, threaten
  life everywhere.

~ Scientists have found ways to prevent or cure diseases
  such as measles, chicken pox, and childhood leukemia.

~ Libraries have thousands of books available
  for every child to read.

~ Some children still lack food, clothing, or shelter.

~ Television sets, skateboards, electric toothbrushes,
  computers, microwave ovens, car phones, and over
  one hundred different flavors of ice cream are
  widely available.

Author's Note

Until the sixteenth century, Europeans celebrated the new year on March 25, not on January 1. In March, days grow warmer, leaves begin to appear on trees, and the first spring flowers bloom. It was natural for people to observe the new year during this time of growth and rebirth.

However, in 1582 Pope Gregory XIII introduced a new calendar making January 1 the beginning of the new year. Many European countries adopted the new calendar in the sixteenth and seventeenth centuries. England and its American colonies did not adopt it until 1752.

This book takes us up to the year 2000, but the twenty-first century and the new millennium actually begin with the year 2001. The twentieth century includes the year 2000, just as a decade includes the tenth year and a century includes the hundredth year. The year 2000 is considered the best time to celebrate because of the change in numbers.

Bibliography

Baker, Timothy. *Medieval London*. New York: Praeger Publishers, 1970.

Brewer, Derek. *Chaucer and His World*. New York: Dodd, Mead, and Company, 1978.

Burton, Elizabeth. *The Pageant of Early Tudor England, 1485–1558*. New York: Charles Scribner's Sons, 1976.

Caselli, Giovanni. *The Middle Ages*. New York: Peter Bedrick Books, 1988.

Durant, Will. *The Story of Civilization: The Age of Faith*. New York: Simon and Schuster, 1950.

Ehrlich, Blake. *London on the Thames*. Boston: Little, Brown and Co., 1966.

Foster, Genevieve. *Abraham Lincoln's World, 1809–1865*. New York: Charles Scribner's Sons, 1944.

Gies, Frances, and Joseph Gies. *Life in a Medieval Village*. New York: Harper and Row, 1990.

Harrison, Molly, and O. M. Royston, comps. *How They Lived*. Oxford, England: Basil Blackwell, 1963.

Hart, Roger. *English Life in the Eighteenth Century*. New York: G. P. Putnam's Sons, 1970.

Hartley, Dorothy. *Lost Country Life*. New York: Pantheon Books, 1979.

Hilton, Suzanne. *The Way It Was–1876*. Philadelphia: Westminster Press, 1975.

Holmes, Martin. *Elizabethan London*. New York: Frederick A. Praeger, 1969.

Huizinga, Johan. *Waning of the Middle Ages*. New York: St. Martin's Press, 1924.

McGovern, Ann. *If You Lived in Colonial Times.* New York: Four Winds Press, 1964.

Morton, Harry. *The Wind Commands.* Middletown, Connecticut: Wesleyan University Press, 1975.

Oakes, Catherine. *Exploring the Past: The Middle Ages.* San Diego: Harcourt Brace Jovanovich, 1989.

Parry, J. H. *The Discovery of the Sea.* New York: Dial Press, 1974.

Pease, Robert. *When Grandfather Was a Boy.* New York: McGraw-Hill Book Company, 1973.

Platt, Richard. *The Smithsonian Visual Timeline of Inventions.* New York: Dorling Kindersley, 1994.

Power, Eileen Edna. *Medieval Women.* Cambridge, England: Cambridge University Press, 1975.

Rickert, Edith, comp., and Clair C. Olson and Martin M. Crow, eds. *Chaucer's World.* New York and London: Columbia University Press, 1948.

Routh, C. R. N., ed. *They Saw It Happen.* Oxford, England: Basil Blackwell, 1960.

Rowse, A. L. *The Elizabethan Renaissance.* New York: Charles Scribner's Sons, 1971.

Trease, Geoffrey. *London: A Concise History.* New York: Charles Scribner's Sons, 1975.

Tunis, Edwin. *Colonial Living.* Cleveland: The World Publishing Co., 1957.

Warner, John F. *Colonial American Home Life.* New York: Franklin Watts, 1993.

We would like to thank David Underdown, professor emeritus, Yale University, and Susan Amussen, core faculty member, The Union Institute Graduate School, for their valuable review of this project.
–E.J. and J.D.E.

Published by Charlesbridge Publishing
85 Main Street, Watertown, MA 02172
(617) 926-0329
www.charlesbridge.com

Library of Congress Cataloging-in-Publication Data
Jackson, Ellen B., 1943-
Turn of the century/Ellen Jackson; illustrated by Jan Davey Ellis.
p.   cm.
Includes bibliographical references.
Summary: Children living in Great Britain and the United States at the beginning of each century between 1000 and 2000 A.D. describe their lifestyle at the time.
ISBN 0-88106-369-X (reinforced for library use)
1. Children–Great Britain–Social conditions–Juvenile literature. 2. Children–United States–Social conditions–Juvenile literature. 3. Great Britain–Social life and customs–Juvenile literature. 4. United States–Social life and customs–Juvenile literature.
[1. Great Britain–Social conditions. 2. United States–Social conditions.
3. Great Britain–Social life and customs. 4. United States–Social life and customs.]
I. Ellis, Jan Davey, ill. II. Title.
HQ792.G7J33   1998
305.23'0941–dc21   97-14264

Printed in the United States of America
10 9 8 7 6 5 4 3 2 1

The illustrations in this book were done in
watercolor and colored pencil on Arches watercolor paper.
The text type was set in Sanvito and Times.
The display type was set in Sanvito and Manuscript.
Color separations were made by Pure Imaging Company, Watertown, Massachusetts.
Printed and bound by Worzalla Publishing Company, Stevens Point, Wisconsin
Production supervision by Brian G. Walker
Designed by Diane M. Earley
This book was printed on recycled paper.